# THE ADVENTURES OF KATE & LEO

## SHALOM

Written by Kaycie Fegley & Elyse Leverett

# HARMONY

## Isaiah 11:6

# REST

Rest is knowing no matter what- God's got you!

## EXODUS 33:14

# PSALM 23

The LORD is my shepherd, I lack nothing.
He makes me lie down in green pastures,
He leads me beside quiet waters,
He refreshes my soul.

He guides me along the right paths for His name's sake.

Even though I walk through the darkest valley,
I will fear no evil, for You are with me;
Your rod and Your staff, they comfort me.

You prepare a table before me in the presence of my enemies.
You anoint my head with oil; my cup overflows.

Surely Your goodness and love will follow me all the days of my life,
and I will dwell in the house of the LORD forever.

# PEACE

May you walk in and with Peace!

PSALM 4:8

# COMPLETENESS

You are complete through your union with Christ, who is the head over every ruler and authority.

## COLOSSIANS 2:10

# SHALOM

Everyone was amazed and gave praise to God. They were filled with awe and said, "We have seen extraordinary things today."
Luke 5:26

# Draw your version of Harmony

# Draw your version of Rest

# Draw your version of Abundance

# Draw your version of Peace

# Draw your version of Joyful Wonder

**Elyse Leverett** is a wife and mom based in Florida. She is passionate about raising up children to know Yahweh intimately and to explore the mysteries all around them. Her hobbies include spending time outdoors, sewing, cooking, traveling and gardening!

**Kaycie** is a native Floridian. She lives to express the heart of Yahweh. She enjoys traveling (including road trips!), dancing, and spending time with friends and family.

The Adventures of Kate & Leo
Written and illustrated by Kaycie Fegley and Elyse Leverett

Copyright © 2021

All rights reserved. This book is protected by the USA, UK and international copyright laws. This book may not be copied or reprinted for commercial gain or profit. The use of short quotations or occasional page copying for personal or group study is permitted and encouraged. Permission will be granted upon request.

All rights reserved. No part of this book, artwork included, may be used or reproduced in any matter without the written permission of the publisher.

Cover designed by Freepik.

Published by Seraph Creative in 2021

ISBN: 978-1-922428-21-9 (print)

www.ingramcontent.com/pod-product-compliance
Lightning Source LLC
Chambersburg PA
CBHW050759110526
44588CB00002B/54